Alpha Zulu

ALPHA ZULU

Gary Copeland Lilley

AUSABLE PRESS
2008

Cover art: "Television," by Jacob Lawrence
© 2007 The Jacob and Gwendolyn Lawrence Foundation, Seattle
Artists Rights Society (ARS), NY

Design and composition by Ausable Press
The type is Goudy.
Cover design by Rebecca Soderholm

Published by
AUSABLE PRESS
1026 HURRICANE ROAD
KEENE, NY 12942
www.ausablepress.org

Distributed to the trade by
Consortium Book Sales & Distribution
The Keg House
34 Thirteenth Avenue NE, Suite 101
Minneapolis MN 55413-1007
(800) 283-3572 (orders)
(651) 221-0124 (fax)

The acknowledgments appear on page 81 and constititute a
continuation of the copyright page.

Library of Congress Cataloging-in-Publication Data

Lilley, Gary.
Alpha Zulu / by Gary Copeland Lilley. —1st ed.
p. cm.
ISBN 978-1-931337-38-0 (pbk. : alk. paper)
I. Title.

PS3612.I42A79 2008
811'.6--dc22
2008010418

To the Stain and Chicago Wally,
thanks for advising, reading, and giving the love.

ALSO BY GARY COPELAND LILLEY

Black Poem (chapbook, 2005)

The Subsequent Blues (2004)

The Reprehensibles (chapbook, 2004)

ALPHA ZULU

I.

Alpha Zulu   *1*

The Mary Magdalene Ceremony   *3*

Anonymous   *4*

Revelle   *7*

Funeral   *8*

Wahtuh   *10*

Submarine Patrol: Mid-Watch Entry 01 JAN   *11*

The Deep Dive Epistle of Watch Section 3   *13*

Ranter on the Corner of Babylon and Manhattan   *14*

Unmarked Grave   *16*

Still Life With Dome Light   *17*

Ratfishing   *18*

Porno   *20*

It's About the Ponies   *22*

Erzu-Lee Enters Mustang Sally's Drag Bar   *25*

My Mother Asks, Will It Kill Me?   *26*

Cicada   *28*

II.

The Charm City Tarot   *31*

III.

Serial   *43*

IV.

Gatesville, Joe Sears' Place   49
Black Poem   50
The Temperature at Which Blood Flows   51
Wake for James Kingsbury of Prince Hall Masons   53
American Rapture at 13 Degrees   54
From the Pile of My Regrets   55
. . . Like a One-Winged Angel Flying to The Lord   57
A Correctional Facility Lesson on What Integrity Is   58
Boneman   59
Shaheed Gives Another Reason Why He Loves Lisa   60
Angels in the Geek Hour of Morning   62
All Praise to the Screwface   64
The Dismal Swamp Just a Few Miles North of Home   65
A Woman Wearing Red   67
Penitence at the All Local Calls Fifty Cents
        Confessional   69
November 11: Veterans Day at Rite Liquor Store
        & Bar   71
Solace   73
Revival   75
Chicago Noir   77

Acknowledgments   81

I.

ALPHA ZULU

I know more people dead than people alive,
my insomniac answer to self-addressed prayers

is that in the small hours even God drinks alone.
My self-portrait: gray locks in the beard, red eyes

burning back in the mirror, the truths of grooves
and nicks on my face, one missing tooth.

I'm a man who's gathered too many addresses,
too many goodbyes. There's not much money

or time left to keep on subtracting from my life.
Except for needs I can pack everything I have

into my old black sea-bag. *To all the bloods*
I'll raise a bourbon, plant my elbow on the bar

and drink to the odds that one more shot
won't have me wearing a suit of blues.

I'm so exposed, with you all of me is at risk,
and if that's only one side of being in love

that's the one deep down that proves it.
Here you are sleeping with me, narcotic as night,

naked as an open hand, and the skinny of it is,
what makes you think I am afraid of this

when I once lived in a cave, moss on the cold wall,
all my bones scattered across the floor.

THE MARY MAGDALENE
CEREMONY

It's the first moment, the touch of water
when an addicted woman can forget.
She is no longer sick at the sink

between street and towel in the bathroom,
but in green hills where she hears one crow
calling sun to the tree. A cool air moves

the bush, all the secrets of crevices
and rocks are exposed. The water running,
she splashes a hand into the valley,

the misdemeanors and felonies fall
into the mirrored lake and what remains
is offered, a blessed less than perfect light.

ANONYMOUS

Pap, my father's old man drove a mule cart
hauling firewood to every liquor still
and wood-burning stove, to every place
that had a warm morning, leaving ruts
on the shoulders of the road.

Gran would drag us all single file
behind her steady step, cleaned
and pressed, marching to Zion.
Yes-Ma'am, my mama's mother, was a teacher
in the Negro school, the Eastern Star
singing to us from the choir loft.

Grandpa was an itinerant preacher
who couldn't read and when he wasn't tending
his own crop he could be found standing
on the corner of a walking distance town
holding his Bible upside down
and always hollering.

One great uncle shot a juke-joint friend
and killed him. A drink, a dance,
and a woman. Caught the bus to the city,
became a minor prophet and a successful
card-playing waiter.

Pap stopped driving a mule cart
when the shoulders on the road narrowed
and woodstoves were replaced by gas.

4

The youngest boy joy rode a car,
got two years, judge offered a choice.
He gave me his dog and went to Nam
and died. His flag is folded and boxed.

Zion was renovated, the choir amplified,
and the old hymns were no longer sung.
Grandpa's last days were spent
quietly sitting in the garden.
My aunt did hair, opened a salon
and pressed my sisters free.
Now her daughter does braids
and my sisters wear kente
but my aunt still styles the old folk.

Another uncle went through college
working a part-time job. Got a business
degree and a vacant lot, and now
he makes good money selling used cars.

My folks met at The Blue Star Club
and he took her home when it closed.
A mile from Yes-Ma'am's door
the gospel they were slipping on
was sliding better with bourbon.
They married at 17, it seemed
they'd been married forever.

The oldest grandson is 26, a homeless
college-educated advocate
for those who hear voices.
He speaks of mud-people giving him truths
and calls for the fall of the wicked
to carpet the walk of the almost-righteous.

He takes donated clothing and any work boots
that he can wet and wear and customize
to the changing shape of his crusty
and swollen feet.

His sister roams the Sunday streets
looking for him. Among the legs of sleeping men
she drops bottled water, she drops blankets,
she drops pairs of socks.

REVELLE

Waiting on Sugar's back step
for the shine. The best known
liquor in the dry county
and the ramshackle Baptists
come to dance in her roadhouse.
The music, the sweet-talk
was spilling through the door,
a clink of ice in a glass
and then Revelle was there,
watching me, a sheen
of dance sweat on her face.

"Boy you ought not be looking
at me like that while sitting
on these steps. Ain't no telling
what kind of trouble you might
be getting your ass into."

They say some men are jukeboxes
of drinking songs about her.
The woman everybody wants
walks on both sides of the road.
The list of her lovers runs long.
I stood up and saw my body in her eyes,
but I did not move up the steps
'cause she dances days and nights here,
with gun-toting Sugar, idling her time
in that whiskey woman's arms.

FUNERAL

for Michael Andrew Lilley

Through tight brick towns
across asphalt beaches
my heart weedy and littered
roadwide pain hounding
whore highways north
like a prophet proven false
by the news of your death.

Deliver us sweet Christ

I have broke bread
with whoever was hungry
and now I pray for you
crossing the state lines.

When our feet of stone stumble

A loaded weapon
and I sweat the fever
my hands tremble
like demons and I thirst
one bourbon my savior
in this death-damned dawn.

And the soul is a sack of sand.

I've improvised a fitful bed
along an obscene wall
but I can not sleep
like a dead house
boarded up and bare inside
when I still hear your steps
in the sand on the sidewalk.

WAHTUH

A summer storm shot across my luck,
the machine voice, the flat palm of a woman
on weed, motor oil, and persistent rumors.
To cool my ear I'll need a river.
Such a mean sky, a dizzy lick,
a thrill-time garden of ricochets,
that ecstatic carnival urge, her gracious giggle
when we leave the road through a tunnel of trees
on Johns Island, South Carolina.
Longing to be a good night tingle lizard
hitting thermal shots straight up,
I drive through her rain and mud
then we're holding close on a porch rocker,
she's back and forth, calling me in the Gullah.

SUBMARINE PATROL: MID-WATCH ENTRY, 01 JAN

*(the first entry of the year is traditionally written in the
ship's log as a poem that details the operational status)*

When we sailed from Portsmouth, New Hampshire
there was a cold dense fog coming off the river.
Line handlers topside were cautious of the ice
on the curve of turtleback aft of the missile deck.
A slip into the freeze would see a man drowning
before this ship could stop. We deployed the day
before New Year's Eve and I know this loneliness
will mark my year. I'm always amazed
how twenty-four hours submerged narrows
the focus and syncopates me with machinery.
I'm on Zulu time, a patrol the next two months
trying not to remember the trace of perfume
in our bed, the way you're there when you've gone
and I wake in the sun-touched room.
An old tradition, the New Year mid-watch entry
must be the pulse of the crew. So I scan
the collective soul of this steel ship
and one hundred fifty squids.
Our course is one four zero, ahead full
at a depth of two hundred feet. Rigged for red.
We have no contacts. Only watch standers
in blue coveralls have their minds completely
on the ship. The sailor's life is buzzard luck
and the most obvious read for me

is the crew's lounge, not one man
shuffling a deck of cards. A new cycle
starts tonight, so I'll take no chances,
anger no gods and I'll try
not to think of you too long.

THE DEEP DIVE EPISTLE OF
WATCH SECTION 3

Lester Yates, your blow-up doll
should have stayed in port.
We are tired of seeing your date
in front of the scheduled flick,
and sitting in the crew's mess
when we're eating chow.
The gapped washable mouth
and her insensitive green eyes
deaden every fantasy in our heads.
We have taken and deflated her.
If you expect to see your friend again
you will do exactly as we say.
If you buck against anything
we'll send you her limp left leg.
You are to get 3 packs of cigarettes,
one of which will be menthol,
and one unfiltered. Leave them all
by the anchor housed indicator
and then walk the submarine
from torpedo tubes, aft, through control,
missile mid-level, past the reactor
and into the heat of the engine room.
Wait at the shaft wearing nothing
but skivvies and a dosimeter.
Try not to sweat into the deck
and we will contact you there
with further instructions.

RANTER ON THE CORNER OF BABYLON AND MANHATTAN

I believe a little harder now GOD is readable the
only distance learning international management
is the city really safer in response watch please I
lived for a reason war is grace staying alive and re-
ligious combat the art of the dead honoring ether
for political paralysis the prairie found a charmed
life I am not in a dream sequence amazing side-
walk spirits what you can do GOD you got the
Sunday 357 you got the edge walking famous leap
year babies all God's children got found traditions
and bushels of burning chads look how they run
amuck in front of God's annoyed hands freaks
and space treats with eight stomping feet venture
for I believe in good the deep GOD the lifeline the
silver sands day jams favorite things and an empty
house is furnished jumble painless GOD zone bet-
ter heard than seen the truth moment side effects
payoffs I got history on a deadline I got hell fear on
ice please visit the attacks don't leave without the
word listen to your cell phone tell me whose voice
it was called our heroes home GOD almighty vio-
lence death is your duct tape stop stop the devil's
in a fury condom nation GOD the whole world
of Gonzo gives a memorial then take a closer look
and a date is the date the stakes the many avenues
of animal care at the wreckage watching GOD

points your coke-filled nose to real opportunity
ground zero rushed-out schemes the damned the
look-alikes foam boxes choke the site breathe va-
porized people my strict policy is ask your doctor
it is the beginning this power that haunts the hard
knock we have with Godfather green pastures
that vary we are lost again with our global track-
ing lost again hope going and nothing feels certain
but GOD you are called my bigger engine my big-
ger trigger business first class mail idol a reply to
the rest the rubble the rabble unlucky ghosts in
the tower of babble this mocked world still reeks
of bravado but jet-fuel lights when GOD has left
the building.

UNMARKED GRAVE

Old man, if it'll help you rest, the shotgun
that has gone from first son to first son

did not come to me, but I do wear the epitaph
of one of your old suits. I remember we stood

in the order of our birth years, children
of the children you left, all holidays

waiting the big Buick to pull in the yard.
For those meals of ash, now you have no stone.

I remember how much you drank and cussed.
Pistol, you burned your people like a torch.

A weed stalk is the devil's walking stick,
the bastard, I know it matters to you

that none of your blood will bring a flower
and nobody but me will cut this grass.

STILL LIFE WITH DOME LIGHT

Look at them glowing around the payphone
by Abraham's store, like three chicken wings
with mumbo sauce, ghosting like stolen cars
with busted back windows and broken lights,
yesterday's newspaper being resold,
dark spaces inside a tattoo parlor.
I know that they've spotted me, nobody's
going to touch a stash until I'm gone.
Makes me want to spread their cheeks on the curb,
hands interlocked on top of doo-ragged heads,
all the custom-fitted ball caps tossed in
the storm drain. Into the piss stank down-flow
where they should be. I want to hold them there
all night, while crackheads stumble up and leave.

RATFISHING

Raven who is also Raymond
found the peepholes the new guy
that rides the bike had drilled
through her bathroom wall so obsessed
to see the tool and a rack of tits
that he was telescoping Raven
from five different positions.
So rather than cut the fool
Raven complained
to the resident manager Lloyd
who tells everyone he's 57
but is really 72. He used to warm
horses and move decently across
a black guitar keeping it slung low
vibrating like a night's nothing
without a pair of hips and then
the Virginia stables burned.
He saved some thoroughbreds
and he has the scars
the cooked skin on his thin legs
make a long walk to his red Buick
parked in front the building
down to the last miles now
and leaking into the stain.

But Lloyd was busy drinking
on the steps with Marshall
his longtime ace who's at least
as old as him and he's got this
almost forty big-butt girlfriend
even though he contends that blonde
black women are dangerous.
Then Brenda's son
got mad and called her a whore
in front of everyone and Lloyd says
every woman in the building
and half the damn men
done sold some ass.
Told the boy don't be too hard
'cause how the hell he think
she raised him to get old enough
to hustle drugs.
But nobody offered
much of any response
on the peepshow so Raven got pissed
greased her face with Vaseline
downed a few long necks
and now it's Raymond
who's waiting out front
for the new dude to get home.

PORNO

Marlboros and distractions, that's what makes
sailors cross the state line, from Portsmouth to
Kittery on foot in the freeze, snow knee deep.
That's not enough to make them cross a frozen
lake, with nothing but the sounds of their single
file steps scratching into the holiday season. Peo-
ple get lonely. Cabs ain't even running, but sitting
in the middle of the theater, in the flicker of Ta Ta's
Triple-X Friday night feature, two swabs from the
shipyard in their civilian jeans and foul weather jack-
ets. Haircuts high and tight. They space an empty
seat between them. They pass a pint through the
opening scenes of the mouths and breasts and
bushes working the long roots, and now they
notice the stained men scattered in the dark, pull-
ing it off, cigarettes and sweat straight ahead into
the show. The squids flash back to the sticky floor
when they walked in. Those salty boys don't sit
there so loose after that, but submarine sailors,
they don't leave while the movie's playing, with
women spread out like a tablecloth, waiting on the
money shot. This gathering of jerked hardheads
ain't enough to keep them away from cinema tits
and ass. This won't be nothing but watch-talk on a
warship, just something to pass the red-light nights
underneath the sea, but there are some truths these
young sailors from the yards don't know yet: that

20

loneliness depreciates with age, that a bad woman is less faithful than the girl on screen, and that every other johnson in the place already knows these things.

IT'S ABOUT THE PONIES

I'm at the racetrack with Zoot
and we're both drinking coffee now
because the bourbon has us down

and he doesn't like how I bet
so I make the run and buy us
two grande Styrofoam cups.

I take the long shots black with sugar
he reads the racing forms
and tracks how the local ponies ran

the past four Fridays at Pimlico.
He contends good horses only lose
when the jockeys stop whipping them

so he digs slap-happy drivers and always
checks to see who's holding the reins
and I say I like my horses smiling.

Plus he's wearing his racetrack clothes
a slick-as-shit blue pin-stripe suit
and his Tio's gray fedora that he stole

while paying respect at the wake.
Got on a pair of one size too small
highly-glossed blue alligator knobs

he found in a thrift shop in New Orleans.
He puts the polish on himself
because he's too tight-fisted

to pay someone else to shine them.
And here I am in black Wrangler jeans
a cotton shirt with holes in the sleeves

looking like the all-day sucker
but a hundred bucks to the good.
It's obvious he doesn't like my smile

and when I try to make small talk
he says if I can't shut my mouth
I might as well just change my seat.

You'd think I'd said something bad
about John Coltrane who's on
a gold medallion dangling off his neck

like it's some type of racetrack crucifix.
He's chewed down to the last three inches
of his Cuban cigar, his left eye

half-closed in the stogie smoke
that creeps up the side of his face.
He's a man of bad habits and he's as mad

as the first wife of a bigamist
because I've won more money than him.
He's a riot sipping his black coffee quiet

while keeping his half-eye off me
and that's the look that has me worried
because he might not drive me home

on account of my gambling approach
lacking horse logic or player sense.
He gets pissed when he discovers

I'm a sorry ass who can't remember
the damn horse's name
and his good eye slams shut in disgust.

The cigar stub glows on one side
of the mouth while he spits
from the other telling me

that I'd won the money
in the third race with El Diablo
on the ride just whipping the hell

out of Lucky's Paradise.

ERZU-LEE ENTERS MUSTANG SALLY'S DRAG BAR

The sharpest knife in the drawer
can't cut a deck no deeper than her.

Blessed queen of hearts in pearls and jeans,
hoop earrings, a bracelet of tattoos,

a blouse you can almost see through
and those stripper shoes. A sweet water flows

across the floor and banks against a gambler's leg.
The luck struck player clears his throat,

hides his next card in the hole,
parks his red deuce and a quarter in the pot,

tells the sweet girl to come sit by his side
and to order any drink she wants.

MY MOTHER ASKS, WILL IT KILL ME?

I'm claustrophobic. I've made
eight submarine patrols
and this was a truth I knew
after the first four. I won't live
in a basement apartment. I find
no comfort under low ceilings.
At sea if I went more than two weeks
without sleep I'd take blue pills
that would let me wake
alert enough to respond to alarms,
casualties, and drills.
I can't stand being contained.
I told my family I don't want to be buried.
Consider that I'll have consciousness
after death, sealed in a coffin.
I know how steel sounds under pressure.
I know what depth it begins to sing.
There are valleys at sea, deep enough
to crush us, the ship gives a tone,
a hum when the hull starts to compress.
You think you're seeing the plates move.
It starts low but the whining of steel
gets louder as a submarine dives.
I want, I say, to be cremated.
Name someone else in this family
besides you, my mother says,

Who'd choose to be in hell twice.
It's ashes that will inherit the earth.
A scattering of ashes? That's an odd fit
for this family's funerals,
someone leaves, we lay the body
beneath their stone.
We're in the church cemetery
on Low Ground Road
and I've just poured libation
beneath our evergreen.
The family plots are in its shade.
She's right, I know
that I will be with them
in my purgatory
of a hole in the ground.

CICADA

Lola and Webster, looking straight ahead,
living color, through the news-box window.
Psalm of the cicadas, incessant buzz
of media news that has followed Katrina
to this dap of sunlight in the Asheville
woods, a sash of red tape, front page above
the fold, the daily song, their loss of home.
The dark suit and donated dress. God snatched
this old man and woman from everything
but each other, and blessed them to have just that.
A peep of red flowers in the woodchips
and weeds by the door of their motel room.
Miles down the road, a disembodied drone,
a 'dozer, a dreadhead at the controls.

II.

THE CHARM CITY TAROT

A ten card spread

King of Swords

Don't believe all those wet-finger stories
caught in the fine hairs of your ear hole.
Even in the part-truths there are salvations.
Do not assume I've screwed every woman
in the phone book just 'cause I'm old school.
I'm the king of tension, the sharpened knife,
but my hand is not on a Glock
looking for no fool, got no cocked hot trigger
waiting on my pull. That's your eight-track,
your Coupe De Ville, rolling midnight
from the District to north-side B'more.
You can't see the problems smoking a spliff,
turning out the lights with Teddy Pendergrass.

Three of Cups Reversed

In the parking lot she's washing her car,
bending down to wipe the rims.
Wide butt and showing waistline, always
some man wanting to wax her trunk.
Sitting on my back porch in a lounger
that's chained to the cast iron railing
I turn obstacles into stepping stones.
Dispel the negative and focus
on the self that hangs off my bones.
Beneath a ragged flag, the bare trees
in the departing winter, ashtray half full,
fresh pack of cigarettes, and three cans of beer
sweating beside me on the table.

Justice

We make our own small mercies.
Reason looks good in boots; the bottle
blonde of dark roots and empathy
mediates and no dispute important enough
shall go unmentioned. Patient listening
and even-handed answers do more
when my woman is telling me
that we are not going to be together
and everything is still cool.
I have to consider myself in concerns
of the heart, and have the final say
about when to leave the city.
I will have to leave the city.

The Hanged Man

I was a long night past being sober. I was
almost bullet-proof, when I made the wish
to stop drinking, getting tattoos, and eating
fried foods. Three fish in the skillet on my stove,
heads to tails, popping in the olive oil,
the scorned woman hot sauce waiting on the shelf.
And I considered giving up smoking
the non-menthol filter tips I've packed around
for thirty loyal years. All my black clothes,
bundled dreadlocks, sacred antenna to God
that I'd cut from my head, I offered to the fire.
I swore to sacrifice patchouli oil, and the balm
for my left shoulder when it's cold in Baltimore.

Four of Swords

Personal history is the real root
of clarity, whose memory can I trust
but my own? The alley behind the house
is often better lit than the street.
Recall what was revealed inside the walls,
everyone adapts to change; the night guards
easing up as the day crew counts
before dawn, prophesy of the bars, spit shined
boots, small eyes, the knife scar
down the cheek of the sergeant, the smell
of coffee coming through the block,
spry young cons waiting on morning chow
talking about swaps of fatback for toast.

The Star

My first day on the mountain, a woman
sits with me on a porch swing, talking
about the voodoo gods getting into her
unfinished novel without her knowing,
and how the night before her car was full
of small white moths even though the windows
were closed. Then she speaks about having breast
reduction when she was 16 and I ask her
what size the girls are now. She just leans
them into me, saying she tells all her new lovers
about it because if they kiss along
the crease they'll see a trace of the knife
and may wrongly think of augmentation.

Six of Wands Reversed

Ain't got the time for crazy shit,
put this pistol in your pocket
before we step. You get no bullets
because you're certain to trip
and shoot somebody and all we want
is the money. I'm going to keep
the loaded piece. I'm the better
shot and I'm going to look out for both
of us. No discussion. I have no love
for the department of corrections.
This is the last time I'll do anything
with you and I don't want no blood,
I don't want no police.

Five of Pentacles

The foundation my grandmother built,
the kitchen was an un-squared room,
dinner at the Formica table, a fifth of scotch
for a centerpiece, the spirits jumping
into the conversation, my Aunt Marcella's oracle
the day before she gave me the white car,
pouring me a cup of coffee and chicory
in the last place I could call home.
Have you noticed, she asked, that the stronger folk
continue to work in the hottest part of the day?
And when it comes to those hard deeds done
by righteous people and martyrs,
isn't it about time for that to be you?

Nine of Wands

I saw them again in the winter tonight,
wrapped in blankets, looking like Bedouins,
drop cloths and tarps billowing, a tent
with floors of cardboard over steam grates
near the subway stop by the monument.
Their shopping carts parked like buses
just waiting for a tourist with a Polaroid.
I drift to sleep and rig for red, the Jonah cast
from a submarine, and I'm sitting on front steps,
cool air that hums with teaser questions,
kids down the street chanting hip-hop rhymes,
my pit-bull pup rolling in the grass,
and my first wife standing sensuous at the screen.

Death

The black cat, someone had tossed
something on him, boiling water
or a chemical cleaner, hitting him along
the flank, leaving a large pale swatch
of bare skin. For two months he stalked
the alley slinking low and close
to the fences. But now he has new growth,
a darker patch in his coat, and he's in front
of the house, stretching and yawning
in the sunlight, and spraying every bush
like this whole neighborhood belongs to him—
every yard, each chicken bone, all vacant houses,
and any female that struts her heat.

III.

SERIAL

1. *Practitioner of the Faith*

I am perilous, baby.
Every day I shave
I say that to myself.
Everything is cut to the stone
of purity, anything less
just gets cut.

2. *Glory*

God is still in business
and the purchase of grace is virtue.
The abundance of His love
follows prayer and cleansing,
a sacrifice by the petitioner.
I stand naked before God. This blade
of tempered steel will be drawn
across the calves.

3. Convergence

If people had seen us pissing
in a halogen alley off 5th Street,
they would have said we were intimate.
I'm wetting the base of the wall,
she squats a shadow length away,
a begged cigarette dangling off her lip.
We're watching each other,
bareheaded and exposed, our steam
coming off the bricks.

4. Her

A cold sliver of moon.
I decide to let the woman
do what she does and then
take back the twenty
I had folded into a cross.
I'd opened it flat and laid it
in the burns of her right hand.
I can smell hell-smoke
in the whore's clothes,
decay in the spread of her skin.

5. Skull

In a vacant house she's wrapped
around me, her head lying
on her balled-up pants. Her hips
grind against me, a dry dance
across my bones. She stares up
at the cracked ceiling, turns away
like I was trying to kiss her,
showing me a side of mouth,
the drug heat chapping her lips.

6. Less Than

It's not a completely random thing,
the impersonal exactness
of the transaction
that buys every hole she has.
When she's finally judged
to be missing, her family will release
an old photograph to the press.
Not many will remember her
ever looking anything like it.

7. Ascendancy

She's a collection
of worn edges
until I push the blade
towards her heart. One hand
keeping God's name
inside her mouth,
I look into her eyes
as she leaves.

IV.

GATESVILLE, JOE SEARS' PLACE

Where every wail and whoop
raises up roadhouse dust
and the one-arm proprietor
skins a smile and cuts a thick cigar
on the real teeth side of his mouth
expertly turning
his pistol hip away from the bar
pouring liquor fast
not spilling a drop and keeping
his bloodshot eye
on everyone.

BLACK POEM

When I sat in back
of Miss Ninth Grade Teacher's
suppose to be remedial class
courting Backrow Debbie
(who I loved more than anything)
ole teacher wanted us
to write poems on how we loves
and feels being black.

Now I ain't never seen
no black poem before
because the books never say
just what shade the thoughts were
and you never know what color
the poem-writer is
unless they say so.

But my hand roam
all over Backrow Debbie.
Across her behind as soft
as the dandelions we'd picked
in the evening summer rains,
and I thought black
must be something nice
to lay down in at night
and forget just how hard the day was.

THE TEMPERATURE AT WHICH
BLOOD FLOWS

I toss a dash of salt in my pot of coffee
    to settle the grounds

by now I suppose he's at that woodpile
    the personal

question that my family does not ask
    my mother is

so proud he's the first grandson
    to do this / walk

a mile to her and split armloads
    of firewood

and kindling every evening this boy
    almost tall as I am

the man of this house and lord
    without trying to

I get mad because he's no mirror I don't
    see myself any

where in him every morning I pray
    remove what pain

comes between us / he works the axe
    'til light fades

gathers the chips in a pail and he goes in
    to my mother's kitchen

where they'll have their cups and talk
    close to the stove.

WAKE FOR JAMES KINGSBURY OF PRINCE HALL MASONS

Parading past his casket does not prove
no one is dead today but him; this lie
telling son-of-a-gun, this unexpected
silent gold-tooth saint, the old man
dressed-up like he's going somewhere formal,
inviting all fierce shaggers to the floor
of the Masonic Lodge. Nobody could
Chicago step like King, he's still the life
of this party, watch the spin and slide.
He's sporting Ray-Ban aviator shades
and it's dazzling to see this daddy-o
whether our reflections be dull or bright.
Everyone in attendance knows his last joke
is the common style of his quiet suit.

AMERICAN RAPTURE
AT 13 DEGREES

Me and my boy are at the wild-card game,
only time I've been in a stadium.
The boss at one of the buildings I clean
gave me 2 tickets, so we're not watching
TV we are in it, close to the field
in the north end zone seats. Our guys score
the winning touchdown on a shuffle pass,
and coming toward us, giving the ball
to my son is the player who'd slanted
inside untouched. You can see every nick
and paint scrape on the helmet, and my boy
is jumping and screaming. The noise
of the frost-bit crowd cannot drown him out,
his passion fills me like I have 2 hearts.

FROM THE PILE OF MY REGRETS

There was no talking them out of it.
The vigilante trip began with us, slipping
in the snow and ice by the old naval prison.
We all used to sit in the rusting cells
and drink jack-black until Krol pulled the lever
one morning and the doors slid shut.
He went to the boat to get his camera for the shot
of Roberts, Tabscott, and me. Like being locked
in a ghost jail at sunrise is a joke to submariners.
Leaving the base in Tabby's blue LTD nobody's armed
with anything but a bad attitude, a beat-down
traveling to Groton to show Roberts you never snitch

and burn one of your own like there's no retribution.
Three pair steel toe boondockers laced tight in the car,
Tabby in the backseat already leaned over drunk
and Krol wanting to get behind the wheel
'cause I wasn't smoking pot or driving fast enough.
"Black ice ain't all that slick," he said, "until you push it
way above the limit, and we got to get there
before the sun comes up, in time to feed
my good boy Roberts *the narc's breakfast.*"
The cold rush of wind riding windows cracked
and then we're waiting an old friend
in our bourbons and black coffees, caught

in the contradiction between the two. Krol on watch
in the parking lot, the cut-off in every good ambush,
Tabscott in a delirium morning sits in the mess hall
both hands holding his cup, not into any small talk.
I wished for the chance to tell Roberts a broken nose
proves you know how to take the straight right hand,
and the black eyes that follow blowing to clear blood
are going to give you hard status, the fighter's mask.
The rapture is when you don't stay down
and the worst you can expect is to wear
the humble mud-hole, the stained white uniform
all informants and fallen saints have worn.

. . . LIKE A ONE-WINGED ANGEL
FLYING TO THE LORD

I could make money in Memphis. I could
sell meals on chrome wheels and own a diner
that specializes in fried-baloney
fried-egg sandwiches served on yard sale plates.
I could chase the rambling dog in the park,
watch the sun sink into the industrial bath.
I could hustle big ass beers on Beale Street
to every cobalt blue poet reading
broken lines drinking on the toxic tour,
sell respirators and bottled water
like a jukebox of Pentecostal songs.
I could become the church that baptizes
in Wolf River while Doris Bradshaw prays
to heal The Depot with faith and wind farms.

A CORRECTIONAL FACILITY LESSON ON WHAT INTEGRITY IS

I can't stand swoll-up bastards always walking the joint with a damn swagger like the clown in the dorm at Lorton, all the time got his shirt off, his iron pile of muscles rippling and him stepping like he's a fallen god when he ain't nothing but a bandit. Pop, the only elder I'd ever listened to, a double-life convict, had a hustle selling cups of coffee and would always tighten me up, and one day I needed one and Pop said he couldn't 'cause that swoll-up asshole had slapped him down and taken all his stuff. God-damn, I got pissed off, gave respect and swore to stick some steel in that son-of-a-bitch. That night he was still prancing when the dorm lights went down and the blue lights came on, before he could get his night vision I was behind him and hit him with the shiv in the side. He didn't know what it was until the second one took him in the lung. He screamed like a pig. The police come and ask me what I know. I say, I know I'm tired of cleaning floors at night but it's my job and I hope I'm doing it good enough. The next morning we went to that bastard's bunk, tore up his pictures and letters from home and dragged his footlocker up to Pop, told him to take anything he wants, and he didn't take nothing but that bag of coffee.

BONEMAN

Don't care who they are
I get paid good to do this
smash the slugger first
against the right hand
and disregard their scream
wait that long moment
then proceed to work
the opposite side both arms
below the elbow my God
you can almost see them
think this is going to be all
and then the left foot I hit it
above the arch my one bit
of mercy I leave the ankle
that's begging for attention
the snap stick bone of the leg
under the knee the shock
by that time usually shuts
the mouth the muscles
of the thigh make a clean
break difficult so I bring
the john henry hard.

SHAHEED GIVES ANOTHER
REASON WHY HE LOVES LISA

A bath takes heat from my body
so I avoid it, hug myself warm,
the crooks of my arms
slammed shut alongside
the bone of my chest because I stink
like a six-day run. I'd come up
with a hundred dollars
and can't remember
where I got it from, but we rode
the sideway seat on the bus
and bought scratch Lotto tickets
just because she had the faith
my hundred could make money.
No feeling beats buying lots
of drugs except smoking it.
But none of that is anything close
to the hazards of those hazel eyes,
the naked looks in them
if she's twisted. On the rush
hour train coming back, a split
three hundred bucks in our pockets,
her tease settling down light
on my lap and making me loose
my long arms to hold her,
shows everyone she's real with me.
and like that I'm a cat-daddy

much better off than them,
because she's my luck
and now is the time
for everybody
to serve
us.

ANGELS IN THE GEEK HOUR
OF MORNING

It's 3 am, Lisa calls Shaheed. In a smoky whisper
she tells him to come get her on 15th Street.
Tells him don't cut the car off and don't park,
and that's exactly what he did. He hit the horn
once and she had her skinny butt in the seat
before the trick could get to his apartment door.

She'd stolen his coat, the tail in the car door
is a minor violation to the leather. The whisper
of worn tires on the Ford. The broken bucket seat
bounces and dances on the pot-holed street
like the radio still plays. Shaheed hears the horn
he pawned and guns the car to Rock Creek Park.

At picnic area # 3 he pulls under the trees and parks,
stands in the dim dome light, in the opened door
where he unzips and fingers himself, playing the horn
for his bashful bladder. The melody is a whisper
in fresh mowed grass. Driving blues bourbon streets
was better with his saxophone in the shotgun seat.

Weary, he walks to the picnic table and takes a seat
in the coolness of dew that has fallen in the park
and softened the traffic sounds from a distant street.
His head in hands, Lisa watches him, and the car door
clicks in the criminal light. *You alright*, her whisper
as she approaches slips easy as a foot on a shoe horn.

Somewhere a blue suit jazzman sits and wipes his horn
backstage, his long legs splayed in front of the seat.
Maybe the music he played is still a whisper
in some woman's good ear, and he'll ask did she park
so he can find her easy when he walks out the door.
Maybe there's an open bar just down the street.

She comes, a sex-for-sale step she uses on the street,
a sultry walk accompanied by the honk of a horn,
one that moves her around to the passenger door
to a good look at the faceless trick across the seat.
She begs a cigarette, gives directions on where to park
in shadows too dark even for a whisper.

Money passes hands like a whisper on the street.
Leaving the park, Shaheed bumps the car horn.
Lisa rocks in her seat, coattail caught in the door.

ALL PRAISE TO THE SCREWFACE

The hustlers, they microscope me
looking for addictions. I know
what they do and why they do it.
I know they don't respect anybody
who'd look into a dope boy's hand
and find a future, like when Mark
sang with a full trash can on his head
for one free rock. Whiskey is a bad road
but crack drives the truck. They laugh
when I say this. I've been spread
on police cars and against walls
more times than I can count the fingers
of their potentially cuffed hands. It gets real
funny when one of them offers me a job.
I'm too old now to be in a red jumpsuit,
with no belt and no shoestrings, sitting on
steel rubbed shiny by the multitudes
of their sliding asses. They speculate
I'm an old dealer out of the game now.
I don't tell them if they're right,
but they always call out and speak
to me with respect when I light a candle
in front of their wall of names.

THE DISMAL SWAMP JUST A FEW MILES NORTH OF HOME

Ain't gotta go where you was,
that's my aunt's advice to me
when she gave me the keys
to the white '87 Cutlass Supreme.
Ten years of her dents, and no reverse.
I drove to DC from Sandy Cross,
along the edge of The Dismal Swamp
where I used to go to get away
from the shattering of the house.

It's about truth. He said
he could recognize the face
he saw in me. I would pull
off the single-lane road
up to the muck and water,
into natural silences caught
in the twisted roots of cypress
to smoke and plan the burning
of this man. Bootleg hoodoo,
and piss swamp water
into the ashes.

Friday nights his truck cooling
in the yard, he sits in the house
until he's drunk enough to cause us
to hide the gun. "Tell Mama."

Some road memory on the radio,
high-beam on the Spanish moss,
the beatings would run through
the weekend. A Sunday deacon,
my mother refuses make-up
and she sits in church in dark shades,
as he prays for someone, maybe
Etta James, to make
everything alright.

A WOMAN WEARING RED

So I picked up the obscene call on the white cour-
tesy phone and asked the party for the number so
I could call her back from the hotel room, and it
was a 1-900 number, which I don't mind, 'cause
everybody got to eat, and then I remembered this
escort gal in Charleston, she wore red Shangri-La
dresses, and had a black heart-of-thorns tattoo
on her bicep, and it's possible I may have loved
her about a hundred years, from the moment she
told me she poured some very heavy whiskey and
then showed me that she did, and she always said
I should taste her home fries which I have not yet
experienced in any of her mornings, but I believe
she's righteous she looks like the whole truth, and
nothing but a real good and necessary lie would
ever come from her mouth, yes, she had a pretty
sweet purr and the right shoes to show her pretty
heels, rode a pair of mules to get your attention,
the kind of woman who could drive you home
even when she's drunk, the gal you look for if
you're coming down a ragged pier after being un-
der the sea for a few months and whatever God
you have grants you some mercy, oh yes, you have
to have the faith that she's there, in all her pleasant
homespun profanities, to bring some damn grace
to your sad sailor life, and you know that she will
notice all of your sutures, all your contusions, and

won't ask 'til it's private because she's polite and near perfect in her pathological ways, so I went down the threadbare hall to my dingy room with the window nailed shut and sat down with yesterday's news, reading the not-so-funnies, wondering how did she know where to find me.

PENITENCE AT THE ALL LOCAL
CALLS FIFTY CENTS CONFESSIONAL

I'm wearing black, with my dreadlocks flying,
a duffle bag of poet clothes. My sister, Ruby,
does not pick up the call. The gang boys
are riding bicycles around the payphone.
I ain't leaving unless things get rough,
and I ain't looking for the law. I rode the train
four days to get here. How do I start?
I gave my mother a gun, a Smith and Wesson
Combat .22 Magnum with a nine shot cylinder
and a heavy frame. The extra weight
made for balance, accuracy. That pistol
was a good fit for her hand. My mother
never married my father but she's been married
two times since. Her second husband, Simon,
the preacher's brother, got upset because I didn't act
like I needed his permission to be in the house.
He's just my mother's husband. I pulled out
a bottle of Jack and drank it by myself
sitting in my mother's kitchen. He quit his job
and burned my mother's house down.
Tossed a Molotov from the yard, got into the Ford
she'd helped pay for and drove off. The folks
on Lowground Road say he was driving
like he'd set himself on fire. My mother lived
on her brother's farm while she cleared the plot
for a double-wide trailer. That's why you don't

see any pictures of us as kids, no trophies,
no awards, no certificates for perfect attendance.
Then last week Simon came back. I didn't expect
to find him lying in my mother's living room,
shot with my registered gun. Everything burns.
Am I to blame for fire? Because of him
there's not one document to prove
me and Ruby even had childhoods, and now
I keep getting her answer machine.

NOVEMBER 11: VETERANS DAY
AT RITE LIQUOR STORE & BAR

Division Street. Nothing like a little bit of blues
and a televised parade to put doom on the hori-
zon. The owner is politely telling José about the
boy, "To me, he is nothing, but he is your son
and you are my friend. Tell him stay out of here
with those gang-bangers. Okay?" Lopez, another
Vietnam vet, pontificates about the mercy involved
in the act of shooting again an enemy combatant
mortally wounded. That's when Mike, who sits
at the end of the bar, asks Lopez the question.
"Hey Loco," he says, "If I give you a million dol-
lars would you do some mercy to this?" He grabs
hold of himself. Lopez fires back instantly, "For a
million I'll do anything you want, you buy me a
drink right now and then we'll talk." The whole
dark bar, about six of us sailors and grunts abso-
lutely crack up. A gut laugh right in the midst of
whatever memories we have of all those who've
died in the boonies and died on the roads. Angel, in
desert chocolate chips and tattoos, a veteran of the
Gulf says, "Are you listening, Mike? I'll even shave
for that million bucks." Then Carla, an ex-Marine,
jumps in, "Forget all that, I'll do it right now for
a hundred, and you better be fast because I ain't on
no mission. If you want the mission, Mike, you'll
have to give me the whole million." And now

even José is picking up his shot and we're all bent over squench-eyed knocking our beers against the bar, everyone laughing hard, so alive and watching Mike go through his pockets.

.

SOLACE

It doesn't cost anything to get high on your hopes. My grandfather never filled up his car, claimed every vehicle he ever drove only broke down with a full tank of gas. I haven't worked in a month and the note is due. Phone bill's on the table beside the water and cable. I don't even look up anymore when the lights start to flicker like Stella Blue, who I first met with the rent party artists in Joe Beasley's third floor loft. She was dancing by herself to bass and drum. A tall woman, wearing long black boots, tight black jeans, and nothing else but a black bra. Not a laundry type of bra, but one of Victoria's nothing-is-secret bras. A black lacy arrangement. It looked like roses were climbing up her trellises, so I stepped towards her. Months later she's telling me how amazed she is that everything is going so fast and so good between us. She thinks back to the night we met and asks what made me approach her. I say, the small lace roses coming across your tits. And Stella Blue didn't like that one bit. She walked out, and I went drinking at a round of bars. I get here at last call and she's on the dance floor half-naked with some other dude. I toss down my drink, peel the hell right out the place, past this squad car parked idling down the street. I turn on the radio and the gospel starts spilling like a prophecy, a consideration on migrating to a Detroit church with pews of prayers. Handclaps transmit a drum beat, a sermon for the blues God, and then, thank you dear sisters, there's the song about our troubles not lasting always.

REVIVAL

On the moaners' bench
some old folks every Sunday
in a storefront of red brick.
Today is worship

and security bars are pulled back.
A black industrial door
with hand-lettered name and address
of the First Missionary Baptist Church.

Half-way down the block a boy
in a big coat assumes the position
by the currency exchange that'll cash
your check and tax you for the privilege

like they're the United States government.
The old folks shake tambourines, stomp
the floor, make their bodies into drums.
Someone opens a song carried for years

in a pocket all the way from the fields.
There's a liquor store, and the Palestinian
owners are afraid in this country now.
This is their turn as aliens of the hour.

Their sons hip-hop like us and work
the Sabbath. Open 18 hours a day.
A crowd lines up for the sacraments
kept behind bulletproof glass:

the booze, the lottery, the cigarettes,
the condoms, candy, and Similac.
The Arabs say they're businessmen
and can't understand why we don't know

in this country about the blood-value of oil.
At the bus stop the hustlers work
beneath a camera that never captures
their images, they believe in the holy stash

of rocks in a balled-up bag.
The narcotics lay beside the garbage can.
The old folks ask blessings
for those sick and afflicted, ask salvation

for their children and grandkids
who do not attend, but today
there is proof the devil is losing, the sirens
cannot be heard inside their hallelujahs.

CHICAGO NOIR (BLUES TRIBUTE TO MOTHERWELL)

Western Ave.: leaving the blue line
I can't name the tune
the National Steel guitar and street traffic
are playing but I remember dancing to it.
Her hip, right side, the near back,
above the waistline a tattoo
of black ink; the shoot of irises
I've held in my hands.

A man doesn't know anything
until he's breathed air at least 30 years—
what he knows then
is that he knows nothing. I am not
the priest of the modern drama
but I can tell you every mistake
I think I've made. My qualified heart
has been going off like a car alarm.

Doctor Feelgood says I may get better,
baby, just not sure I'll ever be well.
I thought this alluring woman was gone.
Gave her logical reasons to leave
a middle-age man. The concern,
she's almost too-much younger,
a million shades of blues have been sung
about being in such a situation.

In the dim golden light of Rosa's club,
during the whiskey solo and complements
of smoke and harmonica,
I lean towards her. She's been waiting
for this and comes to meet me.
The amazing glory of now, our mouths,
just one of her ways in proving
that the main rule of love is to not be dead.

ACKNOWLEDGMENTS

The following poems appeared in the chapbook
Black Poem, Hollyridge Press: "It's About the Po-
nies," "The Deep Dive Epistle of Watch Section
3," "Funeral," "The Temperature At Which Blood
Flows," "Solace," "The Dismal Swamp Just a Few
Miles North of Home," "Black Poem," "Gatesville,
Joe Sears' Place," "Charm City Tarot," "Ranter on
the Corner of Babylon and Manhattan," "Wahtuh,"
"A Woman Wearing Red," "Penitence at the All
Local Calls Fifty Cents Confessional," "Revival,"
"November 11: Veteran's Day at the Rite Liquor
Store and Bar," "My Mother Asks, Will It Kill
Me?," "Chicago Noir," and "American Rapture at
13 Degrees."

The following poems appeared in the chapbook
The Reprehensibles, Fractal Edge Press: "The Mary
Magdalene Ceremony," "Anonymous," " Bone-
man," "Penitence at the All Local Calls Fifty Cents
Confessional," "Ratfishing," "Porno," "Shaheed
Gives Another Reason Why He Loves Lisa," "A
Correctional Facility Lesson On What Integrity Is,"
"Still Life With Dome Light," "Unmarked Grave,"
"Angels in the Geek Hour of Morning," "All Praise
to the Screwface," "The Dismal Swamp Just a Few
Miles North of Home," and "Serial."

Thanks to the following journals, which first
published the following poems:

Heartstone: "The Mary Magdalene Ceremony"

The Bucks County Review: "Revelle"

Milk: "Serial."

Ausable Press is grateful to

The New York State Council on the Arts

The National Endowment for the Arts

The New York Community Trust

for their generous support.

CPSIA information can be obtained
at www.ICGtesting.com
Printed in the USA
LVOW11s0912080817
543828LV00022B/8/P